Going to College

BIBLE READINGS FOR SPECIAL TIMES

...for those times when we want to hear God's word speaking to us clearly

Michael Volland

Text copyright © Michael Volland 2006
The author asserts the moral right
to be identified as the author of this work

Published by
The Bible Reading Fellowship
First Floor, Elsfield Hall
15–17 Elsfield Way, Oxford OX2 8FG

ISBN-10 1 84101 447 8
ISBN-13 978 1 84101 447 0

First published 2006
10 9 8 7 6 5 4 3 2 1 0
All rights reserved

Acknowledgments
Scripture quotations are taken from the Holy Bible, New International Version, copyright © 1973, 1978, 1984 by International Bible Society, are used by permission of Hodder & Stoughton Limited. All rights reserved. 'NIV' is a registered trademark of International Bible Society. UK trademark number 1448790.

A catalogue record for this book is available from the British Library

Printed by Gutenberg Press, Tarxien, Malta

Introduction

I vividly remember sitting with my girlfriend the night before we both left home for university. We spent the evening in the garden of her parents' home with a couple of candles flickering and dripping wax over the wooden table between us. Feelings that were almost too big and profound to put into words filled our heads and our hearts and kept us from saying much. We both knew that in the immediate future our lives would become very different and, although the prospect was exciting, we also felt daunted and full of questions. It was as if a mountain loomed in front of us that we had to climb, without a map.

It was no consolation that we'd had months to prepare, or that we had already got through applications, interviews and waiting for offers. Until that evening, leaving everything familiar behind had always been something that was going to happen in the future. But sitting with Rachel in her parents' garden, our respective bedrooms crammed with boxes full of clothes and CDs and all the precious things that we'd be taking with us to university, and knowing that in just a few hours our parents would be driving us to new places where we would meet new people and do new things, the huge reality of it all hit me with full force.

You are probably excited about your course at college or university. As well as excitement, however, there's a good chance that your head is also full of questions, and perhaps anxieties, about settling into a new place, leaving friends and family behind, meeting new people, fitting in, coping with work and staying on track in your relationship with God.

This booklet has been written to help you identify and think through some of the issues you are likely to face as you settle into an unfamiliar place, make new friends and meet fresh challenges.

Each day you will find a few verses taken from various parts of the Bible. These are based on themes such as loneliness, success, sex and doubt, and are followed by a brief reflection. The idea is that by making time to read, think and pray, you give

God an opportunity to speak to you and challenge you as you start a new life in a new place.

God promises that he will never leave us or let us down. It is true that he is as close to you at college or university as he has ever been. It is also true, however, that your time at college or university is a critical one for your relationship with God. If you so choose, it can be a radical time when you get to know God in a deep and amazing new way. Alternatively, it can be a time when your faith takes a nose-dive.

To a large extent, the way things go between you and God will be up to you. There will be a hundred distractions as you look for a decent church or try to spend time quietly with God, praying and reading your Bible. There will be a thousand reasons not to share your faith or to keep quiet when you have an opportunity to speak up. Keeping your relationship with God passionate, relevant and active is going to be hard work. It's going to require self-control, discipline and time. But you are up for it and you can do it. Make an agreement with yourself and with God that your relationship with him is going to be more committed and more profound when you leave college than when you arrived. Get stuck into reading this booklet each day as a way of making a start, and if something particularly inspires or even irritates you, follow it up. Find other things to read, do lots of talking and listening, and pray hard so that God can show you what is right. Remember that relationships take two, and God wants things between you and him to work out more than you do.

As you leave home to start college or university, have faith in God… and enjoy the booklet!

All Bible quotations are taken from the New International Version.

MONDAY

GENESIS 12:1–3

Facing a new challenge

The Lord had said to Abram, 'Leave your country, your people and your father's household and go to the land I will show you. I will make you into a great nation and I will bless you; I will make your name great, and you will be a blessing. I will bless those who bless you, and whoever curses you I will curse; and all peoples on earth will be blessed through you.'

I switch off when people talk about fractions, so I can't believe I'm about to do it myself. In this case, though, it should make a useful point. God's words to Abram can be divided into two parts: first a set of instructions, followed by a series of promises. The instructions, which by any standards are pretty radical, comprise roughly a quarter of what God says to Abram, whereas the promises of blessing make up about three quarters. Not a bad ratio!

God asks Abram to leave behind all the safety and comfort of home and everything that is familiar to him. God does not even specify the destination. But he promises to bless Abraham and to make him a blessing—to all the peoples of the earth. Abram could not have begun to imagine the scale of what God had in mind when he said that. It is enough for Abram to know that if he sets out as God has asked him to, God will be with him, to bless him and make him a blessing to others. The future was unknown to Abram but he had faith in the God who knows all things.

As you embark upon a new chapter of your life—at college or university—there will be many unknowns. Like Abram, though, you can trust completely that God is with you and that he plans to bless you and make you a blessing to the people around you. And, like Abram, you can't begin to imagine what God will bring to birth in the future as a result of your obedience and trust in him.

Lord, help me to know that you are with me.

TUESDAY

JEREMIAH 29:11–13

Arriving in an unfamiliar place

'For I know the plans I have for you,' declares the Lord, 'plans to prosper you and not to harm you, plans to give you hope and a future. Then you will call upon me and come and pray to me, and I will listen to you. You will seek me and find me when you seek me with all your heart.'

God has plans for you *and* he's told you *and* he's told you what kind of plans. They're good, worthwhile, decent plans, which involve you in reaching your full potential, being kept safe and looking forward to a future full of hope. Knowing that God wants our best should prompt us to seek him and to speak to him wholeheartedly. God loves you enough to make excellent plans for you. Ask him what those plans are. It's guaranteed that they're better than the best plans you could come up with for yourself.

Arriving at college or university, with new friends and new experiences to find, is part of God's plan for you. It is not a shock to God that you are where you are. He isn't thinking, 'Oh no! I didn't expect you to end up here! Not at this college.' We make choices but God directs our steps. He brings us to new places with a purpose in mind—even if it is not immediately clear to us.

Nowhere is unfamiliar to God. God is at work in a place before we arrive and will be there long after we have gone. He knows why he has brought you to the place where you find yourself now. As we were reminded yesterday, God wants to bless us and make us a blessing. God has a role for you to play in the lives of others just as he has a role for them to play in your life. Arriving in a new place among new people can feel daunting, but trusting that God has 'plans not to harm you' can help you to experience his peace and begin to understand more fully why he has led you to this place.

Lord, help me to trust that you have brought me to the right place.

WEDNESDAY

EXODUS 2:15b–17

Who am I now that I've left home?

Moses fled from Pharaoh and went to live in Midian, where he sat down by a well. Now a priest of Midian had seven daughters, and they came to draw water and fill the troughs to water their father's flock. Some shepherds came along and drove them away, but Moses got up and came to their rescue and watered their flock.

Perhaps, in the quietness of these early days at college, you're wondering who exactly you are now that familiar places and people have been left behind and the future is unknown.

In Egypt, Moses had lived in the royal palace. Brought up by the princess, he would have been well educated, well dressed and surrounded by friends. In the passage above, he has left all that behind and finds himself alone in a new place. With his future unknown, Moses was probably wondering who exactly he was.

All of us are products of the home, family and friends we have come from. These are our foundations, etched into our very beings. But foundations are laid to be built on. To mature into the fully rounded person God wants you to be, it is important to move away from familiarity into a new phase of life. Moses' arrival in Midian meant meeting new people and facing tough new challenges from the start. Your arrival at college will involve the same. You are not alone, but among new people, whom God will use to shape you.

All of us are 'work in progress'. As our relationship with God develops, he changes us. When Moses sat down by the well, he was a confused stranger in an unfamiliar place. He could not have imagined himself as the great leader God had determined to make him. As you thank God for the home, family and friends you have left behind, trust him for the person he has in mind for you to be.

Lord, make me all that you want me to be.

THURSDAY

1 PETER 3:13–15

How will people react to my faith?

Who is going to harm you if you are eager to do good? But even if you should suffer for what is right, you are blessed. 'Do not fear what they fear; do not be frightened.' But in your hearts set apart Christ as Lord. Always be prepared to give an answer to everyone who asks you to give the reason for the hope that you have. But do this with gentleness and respect.

Having an active faith in Jesus Christ is going to make an obvious difference to the way you live your life. People will see the fruit of your faith and be intrigued. If some of them ridicule you or exclude you from activities, this shouldn't come as a surprise. And the Bible says that if we suffer for what is right, we are blessed!

Having said this, we should avoid the temptation to seek out suffering as if it somehow impresses God. Suffering alienation from our peers because we haven't been gracious or sensitive with our words is foolish. If we lead those around us to see Christians as self-righteous and narrow-minded, we are not following Jesus' example. Our witness should lead our peers to open rather than close their ears to the message God wants to share through us.

You might be the only Christian on your floor of the hall of residence or in your shared flat, but as you live for Jesus and pray for your friends, God will be at work. When your friends see that you 'do not fear what they fear', they will be curious. This will perhaps be most obvious at times when the pressure is on—when deadlines or exams are looming. As you give your anxieties to God and find peace in him, your friends will want to know what your secret is. Be prepared to give a simple, gentle answer. Think it through now. What will you say to explain your behaviour and introduce your curious friends to the God who made them?

Lord, help me to be wise and gracious among my friends.

FRIDAY

LUKE 5:29–32 (ABRIDGED)

Making new friends

Levi held a great banquet for Jesus at his house, and a large crowd of tax collectors and others were eating with them. But the Pharisees… complained to his disciples, 'Why do you eat and drink with tax collectors and "sinners"?' Jesus answered them, 'It is not the healthy who need a doctor, but the sick. I have not come to call the righteous, but sinners to repentance.'

Arriving at college means a great opportunity to make a whole lot of new friends. If you're going to follow Jesus' example, you'll have to avoid the temptation of only making friends with other Christians. You'll need to be in relationships with people who aren't Christians—and the more the merrier! Clearly it is also essential to have Christian friends whom you love and trust, but in building genuine friendships with people who don't yet know God, you'll learn masses and open up opportunities for God to reach these new friends with his love and mercy.

Jesus went to the banquet at Levi's house and hung out with a whole bunch of people considered to be 'outside' God's kingdom. The Pharisees complained—but they had misjudged God and what it meant to serve him. Jesus tried to help them to see things differently on many occasions but the verse above contains a particularly brilliant example: 'It's not the healthy who need a doctor, but the sick.' Jesus wasn't pleased that the 'sinners' he spent time with were far from God. He went to Levi's house with a message of reconciliation: 'I've come to call sinners to repentance.' Jesus made friends with those who didn't know God and who felt excluded from God's plan, so that he could tell them that things could be different. It is our job to copy his example, and that will involve making a group of friends who don't know God yet.

Lord, help me to see others as you see them.

WEEKEND ONE

1 CORINTHIANS 6:12

Sex

'Everything is permissible for me'—but not everything is beneficial. 'Everything is permissible for me'—but I will not be mastered by anything.

The freedom of life at college offers a thousand attractive possibilities. Sex is definitely one of them. In his grace, God allows us a remarkable amount of freedom; we can choose what to do and with whom. Alongside our freedom, God provides guidance so that we can understand how to use our freedom in the best way possible.

The verse above states, 'Everything is permissible for me.' But it goes on to say that this doesn't mean everything is good for us. Sex is a God-given activity that we are designed to do. In its intended context it is an expression of the intimacy that we are all seeking—a demonstration of mutual desire, affection and commitment. In the Bible, God lovingly teaches us that the only context for sex is in heterosexual marriage. Although we are free to engage in sexual activity how and whenever we like, if we do it outside of God's intended context, we will harm our relationship with God and, very probably, ourselves and our partner.

As God is the designer, who knows the intimate and raging desires of our hearts and bodies, we are certainly able to trust that he knew what he was doing when he limited sex to marriage. He is a source of strength and patience when desires frustrate to the point of overwhelming us.

Our sex drive is a powerful force and sex can easily become the central focus of our thoughts. The verse ends by saying, 'I will not be mastered by anything.' It is important not to let anything become more central than God. Sex has a place in God's purposes and, as we ask him, God will show us clearly what that place is.

Lord, help and guide me.

WEEK TWO •

MONDAY

HEBREWS 13:4, 6

Intimate relationships

Marriage should be honoured by all, and the marriage bed kept pure, for God will judge the adulterer and all the sexually immoral… 'The Lord is my helper; I will not be afraid.'

Christians agree that casual sexual relationships should be avoided. Things become a bit greyer, however, when Christians find themselves in an exclusive relationship and feel they've fallen in love. If this is you, doubtless you want to spend all your time with the other person. You talk in depth about everything. You're inspired and excited when you're together. In fact, you feel more yourself when you're together than you do alone. You are committed—perhaps already thinking about marriage and children. You don't want anyone else but you badly want your partner. You want to give your whole selves to each other. You know that God says sex is just for marriage, but that's not practical yet, and you're in love, so what's the problem?

It's an obedience and a trust thing. God indeed says that sex is for marriage. He doesn't provide any small print that says, '… unless you really love each other—then sex before marriage is fine'. If we take God seriously, then we have to take his directions seriously and learn to obey him and trust him.

The verse above says that the marriage bed should be kept pure. In other words, sex is to be kept for marriage and within marriage. If you're in love with the person that God wants to give you, then he is your helper: you don't need to be afraid. And God is faithful—eager to give you both patience, wisdom and grace. God will help you to help each other postpone sex so that you can discern whether this person really is the right one and, if so, to wait a short while until marriage is possible.

Lord, give me patience and self-control.

TUESDAY

HEBREWS 10:23–25 (ABRIDGED)

Christian community

Let us hold unswervingly to the hope we profess, for he who promised is faithful. And let us consider how we may spur one another on toward love and good deeds. Let us not give up meeting together… but let us encourage one another— and all the more as you see the Day approaching.

As a Christian, you have a great hope: God's Spirit is living and working in you now as a guarantee of resurrection to eternal life. Read that again and let the weight of it sink in properly!

The writer is encouraging us to keep this hope at the front of our minds, but he realizes that if it is to make us people who positively affect our world in the name of Jesus, we all need the encouragement of other believers. He asks us to think about the ways in which Christians can spur each other on to 'love and good deeds'. Who is spurring you on to live the Christian life to the full? How are you spurring others on to live God-focused lives?

We are told not to give up meeting with other Christians. If we think we can be a Christian alone, we're deceiving ourselves. Becoming a Christian means being part of the community of God's people, even though we may often find it difficult and frustrating. God calls his people into a community so that they can work at loving, encouraging, teaching and helping one another. If your relationship with God is going to develop into maturity, it is essential to be part of a Christian community.

The verse above also speaks about the 'day' approaching, meaning the day when Jesus will return in glory to judge the world. We have a finite time in which to live for God, and meeting with other Christians is an essential way of making sure that the way we use our time has eternal significance.

Lord, give me the desire to meet regularly with your people.

WEDNESDAY
1 PETER 4:8–10

The Christian Union

Above all, love each other deeply, because love covers over a multitude of sins. Offer hospitality to one another without grumbling. Each one should use whatever gift he has received to serve others, faithfully administering God's grace in its various forms.

An obvious place to find Christian community at college is the Christian Union (CU). Meeting with other Christians is not always easy, but the verse above tells us to 'love each other deeply'. Love helps us to put aside any frustrations we may have and allows us to see others as God sees them. There might well be a few people whom you find difficult or apparently very different from you, but we are also told, 'Offer hospitality to one another without grumbling.' Perhaps it would be worth cheerfully inviting people you struggle with round for a meal or a coffee.

The verses go on to tell us to use the gifts God has given us to serve others. What better place to exercise your gifts than among fellow Christians in the CU? As everyone brings their own gifts, the CU should become a place where faith is able to blossom. It should be a bit like a gym—a place where Christians 'work out' together to get in good spiritual shape for God-centred living.

An effective CU will be a place of fellowship and a platform for mission, not a closed community of content-but-ineffective Christians. If all your friends are in the CU, you will quickly become afraid of engaging with the masses of your fellow students who need Jesus but don't come within a mile of the CU.

Be an active part of the CU, use your gifts to help build it up, but don't let it become a place where you settle in and put your feet up. Get out and make friends who have never heard of the CU!

Lord, give me wisdom and grace as I make new friends.

THURSDAY

ACTS 2:44–47 (ABRIDGED)

Finding a decent church

All the believers were together and had everything in common. Selling their possessions and goods, they gave to anyone as he had need. Every day they continued to meet together in the temple courts. They broke bread in their homes and ate together with glad and sincere hearts… And the Lord added to their number daily those who were being saved.

The verses above describe a pretty amazing church. When you look around at potential churches in your new town or city, you might be tempted to be a little disappointed. Don't despair. God has exciting plans for his church and you are part of them. And being part of God's plans for the church involves being part of a church.

So, where do you start? A great way to begin anything is to pray. Looking for a decent church is no exception. God knows the right place for you and has a church in mind where you can be a blessing as well as being blessed. As you look around at different churches, it will help to ask yourself, 'Is this a church where the people love Jesus, worship God with sincerity, welcome the Holy Spirit, teach the Bible and are trying to live the Christian life in relevant ways so that other people get saved?' If the answer is 'no', it's probably best to try somewhere else.

Bear in mind that church is not about getting a spiritual buzz, having a great social life or meeting a potential partner. Church is about worshipping God with his people, and being equipped to serve him better. Ask yourself, 'Is this a place where I am going to be challenged and inspired and where I will have an opportunity to develop the gifts God has given me?'

It's a massive privilege to be part of what God is doing with his church. There are exciting times ahead, so get stuck in!

Lord, guide me to the right church.

FRIDAY

HEBREWS 11:1, 6

New perspectives and faith questions

Faith is being sure of what we hope for and certain of what we do not see... And without faith it is impossible to please God, because anyone who comes to him must believe that he exists and that he rewards those who earnestly seek him.

Arriving at college with a faith in God puts you in the minority. That doesn't mean, however, that you are among people with no faith. The few atheists you'll meet will have deep faith that there is no God. Many more people will have faith that there must be 'something out there'—they're just not sure what 'it' is. There's no such thing as a neutral, faith-free position. Everyone's view on the really 'big' questions involves faith.

You'll probably find that most people haven't spent much time thinking their views through deeply—but that won't stop them from asking you difficult questions when they discover you're a Christian. It may make you the focus of some pretty tough and well-argued criticism. 'What about other religions? Why does God allow suffering? Isn't religion the root of all war?' Rather than letting these difficult conversations wobble your faith, however, see the questioners for what they are: spiritually hungry people, keen to find out if your faith has any substance.

Today's passage tells us that Christian faith involves 'being sure of what we hope for' (our salvation), and 'certain of what we do not see' (the risen Jesus Christ). Faith wouldn't be faith if we had all the answers. Faith allows us to read about the salvation Jesus won for the human race and to believe it. Of course we must ask demanding questions—the Christian faith has been asking tough questions of itself for its entire history—but ultimately, as the passage tells us, 'without faith it is impossible to please God'.

Lord, help me to strive for an informed faith.

WEEKEND TWO

1 CORINTHIANS 1:18–19, 21b

Faith in a secular academic environment

For the message of the cross is foolishness to those who are perishing, but to us who are being saved it is the power of God. For it is written: 'I will destroy the wisdom of the wise; the intelligence of the intelligent I will frustrate.' … God was pleased through the foolishness of what was preached to save those who believe.

OK, so the idea of a man with a virgin mother being 'the son of God', dying to pay for the sins of the whole world and then coming back to life again does sound a little far-fetched in the context of 21st-century academic life. But, as the passage above says, 'the message of the cross is foolishness to those who are perishing'. For many non-Christians in the West, the idea that the death and resurrection of Jesus provide a way for the human race to be reconciled to God is nonsense.

Clearly this was also the case when Paul wrote today's verses to the church in Corinth. Some who heard the Christian message believed and, by believing, gained life. Others sneered, claiming that superior intelligence and wisdom prevented them from entertaining such foolish teaching. Paul argues that the apparent 'foolishness' of the Christian message is God's way of humbling the arrogance of those who imagine they are more sophisticated.

If you profess faith in Jesus Christ at college, you will risk the scorn of your lecturers and friends, but you can be encouraged by the fact that Paul (who was seriously clever) faced the same difficulties, that God, in his infinite wisdom, is 'pleased through the foolishness of what was preached to save those who believe' and that many well-respected people in the academic world publicly profess faith in Jesus Christ.

Lord, enable me to see the wisdom in your way of doing things.

WEEK THREE •

MONDAY

2 PETER 1:16

Dealing with doubt

We did not follow cleverly invented stories when we told you about the power and coming of our Lord Jesus Christ, but we were eyewitnesses of his majesty.

If it was relatively easy to have faith in God in the secure, familiar environment of home, things can seem different when Christian family and friends are far away. You don't know any Christians, you haven't found a decent church, no one you've met believes in God and they all have great reasons why not. Doubt creeps in and you begin to wonder if Christianity really is 'true'. After all, if you're not feeling anything spiritual and people around you have a contradictory set of answers for life's big questions, the whole thing can seem more complicated and less certain than it used to.

In today's verses, Peter gets straight to the point: 'We did not follow cleverly invented stories…'. He is reassuring his readers that the truth has been told about Jesus. The disciples didn't sit around dreaming up a new religion or planning a big practical joke. Peter tells us that he and the others were 'eyewitnesses'. There really was a man called Jesus, he really did claim to be able to forgive sins and give eternal life, he really was executed and Peter and lots of other witnesses really did see him alive again, walking, talking and eating. These events really happened at a particular point in time and space and *Peter saw them*!

You might well struggle with doubts as you adjust to life at college and are exposed to a hundred conflicting points of view. Doubts are part of faith. As you wrestle with doubt, though, keep returning to God in prayer. Ask him to help you understand. And keep returning to your Bible—remind yourself about what you believe by reading what the eyewitnesses have put in writing.

Lord, guide me through times of doubt.

TUESDAY

MARK 1:35

Prayer (do it...)

Very early in the morning, while it was still dark, Jesus got up, left the house and went off to a solitary place, where he prayed.

Jesus made an effort to get up early to spend time alone with his Father in prayer. He prayed on all kinds of occasions and taught his disciples and followers to copy his example. At the start of a relationship with someone special, you spend hours talking to each other, growing to know each other intimately and value each other. In the same way, our understanding of God and our love for him grow as we spend time speaking and listening to him in prayer.

Not many people find prayer easy. It can be hard to concentrate and we can begin to wonder if we are simply speaking into thin air. Or we wonder if it's worth bothering with at all. Surely, if God knows everything about us, there's no need to speak to him?

God definitely knows everything about us—he made us, and therein lies the point of prayer. Prayer is for our benefit, not God's. God has created us to live in relationship with him, and deep relationships are built on good communication. We have to remember that prayer is something that develops over a lifetime. Speaking with God can be difficult and frustrating but ultimately it is essential if you are to walk closely and effectively with him.

Your times of prayer should sometimes be simply sitting silently in God's presence. During such times, God will whisper quietly to your spirit—challenging you, revealing things to you and changing you. Try following Jesus' example of getting up early to spend time alone with your heavenly Father. You might find that your relationship with God reaches a profound new level as you step into his presence while the world around you is still sleeping.

Lord, remind me to pray, and inspire my praying.

WEDNESDAY

2 TIMOTHY 3:16–17

Reading your Bible

All Scripture is God-breathed and is useful for teaching, rebuking, correcting and training in righteousness, so that God's servant may be thoroughly equipped for every good work.

In the first five words of the verses above, the Bible makes a massive claim about itself. Christians believe that the Bible, although written by human beings, is directly inspired by the Spirit of God. The Bible points to a gigantic cosmic story in which God is the central character and in which you have a significant role.

So how often do you read your Bible? I mean read it properly, not just opening it at random, reading a few sentences, getting distracted and then doing something else. If you want God to speak to you, reading your Bible attentively is one of the easiest ways to allow him to do it. God reveals his character in the pages of the Bible. It's in the Bible that we read the eyewitness accounts of what happened when God took human form and stepped into history. The words and deeds of Jesus are recorded so that we might come to faith, understand how God wants us to live and be inspired to share the good news with others. If you're keen to know what God thinks about something, it's more than likely that he's made it clear in the Bible.

As you discipline yourself to push other things to one side and to read and reflect on passages of the Bible, your understanding of God will make speedy progress. You will often find yourself encouraged and uplifted and you'll discover a reliable source of strength and guidance in difficult times. As you make time to read your Bible, your relationship with God will grow deep and strong as you become 'thoroughly equipped for every good work'.

Lord, help me to fall in love with your word.

THURSDAY

PHILEMON 4–6

Living for God

I always thank my God as I remember you in my prayers, because I hear about your faith in the Lord Jesus and your love for all the saints. I pray that you may be active in sharing your faith, so that you will have a full understanding of every good thing we have in Christ.

Like the writer of today's verses, your family, friends and church back home will be thanking God as they hear that things are going on well between you and God. They will also be praying that you are 'active in sharing your faith'.

Sharing faith is a fundamental part of the Christian life. For people to have the chance to start a relationship with God, they have to hear the story about Jesus. The only way that's going to happen is if Christians like you and me talk about it and live as if we believe it! If you're going to live for Jesus and talk about him, you need to have an intimate relationship with him. As you get closer to Jesus, the way you live and the things you say will naturally start to reflect him and make your friends ask questions.

The verses above make it clear that being active in sharing faith is important for Christians so that we 'have a full understanding of every good thing we have in Christ'. It would seem that through actively sharing your faith in Jesus Christ, your own understanding of what he has done for you will grow and develop.

This makes sense on a very simple level. The more you talk about or do anything, the more questions about it you'll encounter, the more thought you are likely to give it and the more your understanding will naturally deepen. If you are to have a full understanding of what Jesus has done, is doing and will do for you, be active in sharing your faith through your words and deeds.

Lord, help me to share my faith generously and sensitively.

FRIDAY

COLOSSIANS 1:16

Life to the full

By him all things were created: things in heaven and on earth, visible and invisible, whether thrones or powers or rulers or authorities; all things were created by him and for him.

Today's verse tells us that everything that we see, and much more that we don't see, was created through Jesus and for Jesus. God is a prolific creator. If you look around, even right where you are at this moment, it will be obvious that our creator God loves diversity and beauty, has a sense of humour and enjoys surprising us.

It is sad, then, when Christians adopt opposite characteristics. In our attempts at God-centred living, we can slide into being conservative, plain, over-serious and afraid of change or difference. Things are not this way in creation or in the life Jesus modelled.

As the Son of God, Jesus was the ultimate human being. He had no sin. Sin distorts God's creation and prevents us from having a welcoming, creative, fun and broad-minded approach to the life God has given us. But Jesus died to set us free from sin and to enable us to adopt God's approach to living. As we grow into this new way of life we'll naturally lead lives that attract our friends to Jesus. Everybody responds to creativity, a sense of humour, a readiness to engage and have fun, to a person who gets stuck in and enjoys being with and listening to others. These are the characteristics of Jesus, and as Christians we can expect to see them developing in our lives, for our own and others' benefits.

Ask God to help you develop a creative, fun, broad-minded approach to life. Remember that Jesus made and loves the people who hang out in places you might be tempted to avoid as a Christian. Live life to the full, for Jesus. Go where he'd go, do what he'd do and enjoy being who he wants you to be.

Lord, make me everything you have in mind for me to be.

WEEKEND THREE

1 CORINTHIANS 10:27, 31–33 (ABRIDGED)

'Whatever you do'

If some unbeliever invites you to a meal and you want to go, eat whatever is put before you without raising questions of conscience… So whether you eat or drink or whatever you do, do it all for the glory of God. Do not cause anyone to stumble… For I am not seeking my own good but the good of many, so that they may be saved.

Notice that in these verses, Paul does not say, 'If some unbeliever invites you to a meal, don't go just in case you offend God…' He says, if you want to go, that's fine, and when you get there eat whatever they serve up. For Jewish Christians, this meant running the risk of being served prohibited food, but Paul is saying that they should just eat up and keep quiet because, ultimately, they are seeking to glorify God by helping unbelievers to find faith.

You can be certain that your salvation is secure, not because you avoid certain foods or non-Christians or 'suspect' places, but because you have put your faith in Jesus Christ. So whatever you do, whoever you're with and wherever you go, do it with Jesus consciously in the centre of your life and God will be glorified.

At college there will be plenty of invitations to meals, bars, clubs and parties. If someone invites you and you want to go—go! You can glorify God just as well on a dance floor at 3am as you can in church on a Sunday morning. However, Paul goes on to say, 'Don't cause anyone to stumble.' Our actions mustn't cause other Christians to get into difficulties with their faith. You might feel fine about going to clubs and parties, but if a Christian friend has issues with alcohol, drugs or sex and comes along with you, they could end up compromising their faith. For their sake, it might be worth thinking again about where and how you spend your time.

Lord, give me the wisdom I need to live for your glory.

MONDAY

1 TIMOTHY 6:6–7, 9–10 (ABRIDGED)

Measuring success

But godliness with contentment is great gain. For we brought nothing into the world, and we can take nothing out of it... People who want to get rich fall into... many foolish and harmful desires that plunge people into ruin and destruction. For the love of money is a root of all kinds of evil. Some people, eager for money, have wandered from the faith and pierced themselves with many griefs.

Why have you come to college? You might want to deepen your knowledge of a subject that excites you. Your parents may have insisted that, in order to get on in life, you need a degree. It might be that playing a particular sport at a high level for the college or university team is your motivation. You may just have been looking for a worthwhile way to spend three years while you decide what you want to do with your life. Whatever the reason, you have goals and ambitions and dreams about what you might do once you've got your degree.

It feels good to be successful but Paul teaches us that we should be most concerned about making a success of godliness: 'godliness with contentment is great gain'. Being successful at achieving this really matters to God and is the secret of a full and worthwhile life. It is the opposite of trying to get rich—which often leads us far away from God and will cause us all kinds of grief.

Paul reminds us that we can't take anything with us when we die. When you meet God, he won't ask you whether you got a first, or captained the hockey team, or made your parents proud, or got a great job in the city with a big salary. Although these may be important now, what is of eternal importance and immediate benefit is making a success of your relationship with Jesus.

Lord, help me to strive for success in godliness.

--- TUESDAY ---

JAMES 1:2–5 (ABRIDGED)

Use of time

Consider it pure joy, my brothers and sisters, whenever you face trials of many kinds, because you know that the testing of your faith develops perseverance. Perseverance must finish its work so that you may be mature and complete, not lacking anything. If any of you lacks wisdom, he should ask God... and it will be given to him.

Today's passage tells us to ask God for wisdom. As you start college, it's particularly appropriate to ask God to make you wise in the way you spend your time. God knows what is in store for you so he has a good idea about what your priorities should be in the present. He'll give you discernment about what's worth spending time on and what isn't—which won't mean only spending time on things that you really enjoy! The passage talks about facing trials and having your faith tested. God wants us to develop and this won't happen if everything is always comfortable. Today's passage tells us that tough times produce perseverance, which is necessary so that 'you may be mature and complete, not lacking anything'.

All the time you have is given to you by God. We should try to avoid mentally dividing time up between God and everything else. There are no such things as 'God's time' and 'my time'. Of course you need to set aside time in which you are specifically focused on God, but he is still with you when you go off to do something else.

God will hold us all accountable for the way we use the time given to us. Time is precious and God expects us to use it wisely —which is why it is important to ask him for wisdom in this area. God is eager to help you find a suitable balance between studies and relaxation, spending time with friends and time alone with him. Ask him to help you and trust him to deliver.

Lord, direct the way I use my time.

WEDNESDAY

EPHESIANS 6:14–18a (ABRIDGED)

Looking after yourself

Stand firm then, with the belt of truth buckled around your waist, with the breastplate of righteousness in place, and with your feet fitted with the readiness that comes from the gospel of peace… Take up the shield of faith, with which you can extinguish all the flaming arrows of the evil one. Take the helmet of salvation and the sword of the Spirit, which is the word of God. And pray in the Spirit on all occasions with all kinds of prayers and requests. With this in mind, be alert.

Looking after yourself at college will obviously involve things like getting enough sleep (at least a couple of times a week), eating well (pot noodles don't count), taking time off from studying (not too much of a problem) and finding out where the launderette is. These are common-sense things and you don't need someone pointing them out. Not so obvious, perhaps, is the need to attend to your spiritual health. This can go a long while unchecked, and it can be easy to miss the gaps that open up in your walk with God.

One way of staying on top of things is to use Paul's 'armour of God' passage as a checklist. You might not feel connected to the imagery (which Paul drew from his observation of Roman soldiers) but, with a little imagination, the images can be seriously useful.

The six essential items are truth, righteousness, readiness, faith, salvation and the word of God. If we are going to 'stand firm' and lead worthwhile, effective Christian lives, we must consciously take hold of these things each day and 'put them on'. We must add to these a growing desire to 'pray in the Spirit on all occasions' and, crucially, to 'be alert'. Attending to your spiritual health like this is what really looking after yourself involves—even if doing it means never having time to visit the launderette!

Lord, remind me to put on your 'armour' each day.

THURSDAY
JOHN 14:1–3

Homesickness and feeling lost

'Do not let your hearts be troubled. Trust in God; trust also in me. In my Father's house are many rooms; if it were not so, I would have told you. I am going there to prepare a place for you. And if I go and prepare a place for you, I will come back and take you to be with me that you also may be where I am.'

For most people starting college, there will be times when they feel homesick. When you're busy you might not notice it. It's when you close the door to your room and find yourself alone that it can hit you. Everything that was familiar is miles away: parents, siblings, friends, the places you used to hang out, your church. In their place are unfamiliar faces and buildings, streets and shops. The contrast can make you feel lost and deeply alone.

The words in today's verses are Jesus' own. He knew what it felt like to be in unfamiliar places, far from home. He had learnt to trust his heavenly Father and to have a peaceful heart, so he was well qualified to advise his disciples to trust God when he was about to leave them. He knew that they would be worried and upset about being physically separated from him. He also knew that it was necessary for him to go, so he comforted them with words about trusting God and trusting him. These words are as much for you as they were for the struggling disciples.

Jesus goes on to talk about heaven. He reassures his disciples that they will join him where he is going. Again, this is as much for you as it was for them. As a Christian, the only place where you will feel completely at home is with Jesus, in his Father's house. As you adjust to life at college, you may feel lost or homesick, but as you trust your heavenly Father and allow his Spirit to comfort and reassure you, you will find that your heart is less troubled.

Lord, comfort me when I feel alone.

FRIDAY

1 SAMUEL 2:18–19, 21 (ABRIDGED)

Home–independence tension

But Samuel was ministering before the Lord—a boy wearing a linen ephod. Each year his mother made him a little robe and took it to him when she went… to offer the annual sacrifice… And the Lord was gracious to Hannah; she conceived and gave birth to three sons and two daughters. Meanwhile, the boy Samuel grew up in the presence of the Lord.

When he was very young, Samuel was sent away from home to work in the temple. He was the oldest of six siblings. He saw his family once a year when they came to the temple. Most of the time Samuel was surrounded by people who were not his family. He made a life for himself, grew, learnt and developed far away from his mother and father, his brothers and sisters.

It must have been a bit awkward for all of them on that single meeting each year. What do you say to a group of people who, on one level, you are extremely close to—they're your own flesh and blood—but who you hardly ever see? All the experiences that shaped Samuel were happening without his family's knowledge. Samuel and his family must have really struggled—frustrated by wanting to be intimate but spending very little time together.

Things might feel similar for you and your family. As you build a life for yourself at college, however well you keep in touch, most of the time you are doing things that your family know nothing about. This can make things awkward at holiday times when you go from being an independent adult to being asked what time you might be in at night. Bear in mind that it is difficult for your family too. Be patient and gracious and, before you go home for vacations, pray about the time you'll spend with your family. Ask God to fill it with his peace and direction and to make you a blessing to each other.

Lord, help my family and me to love and support each other.

WEEKEND FOUR

PHILIPPIANS 1:6, 9–11

God, you and the future

He who began a good work in you will carry it on to completion until the day of Christ Jesus… And this is my prayer: that your love may abound more and more in knowledge and depth of insight, so that you may be able to discern what is best and may be pure and blameless until the day of Christ, filled with the fruit of righteousness that comes through Jesus Christ—to the glory and praise of God.

God is with you as you start life at college. He is faithful, and is closer than your breath at every moment of each day. He wants to see you become all that you can possibly be. The passage above reassures us that 'he who began a good work in you will carry it on to completion'. God made you and called you into relationship with himself. He is working in you to heal what is damaged and to build up what is good, and he will finish the job he has started. If you never pray or read your Bible or go to church or the CU, God won't give up on you. But you are unlikely to experience all that he has for you because it's through things like these that God moulds us into the kind of people that we can only be with his help.

The passage above speaks about 'the day of Christ'—the day when Jesus will return. No one knows when this will be, but one thing is certain: that day will arrive and you will meet Jesus face to face. With this in mind, my prayer for you as you settle into life at college is the same as Paul's prayer for the Philippians: 'that your love may abound more and more in knowledge and depth of insight, so that you may be able to discern what is best and may be pure and blameless until the day of Christ, filled with the fruit of righteousness that comes through Jesus Christ—to the glory and praise of God.' Amen!

Lord, transform me and keep me focused on Jesus.

Bible reading notes from BRF

If you have found this booklet helpful and would like to continue reading the Bible regularly, you may like to explore BRF's three series of Bible reading notes.

NEW DAYLIGHT

New Daylight offers a devotional approach to reading the Bible. Each issue covers four months of daily Bible readings and reflection from a regular team of contributors, who represent a stimulating mix of church backgrounds. Each day's reading provides a Bible passage (text included), comment and prayer or thought for reflection. In *New Daylight* the Sundays and special festivals from the church calendar are noted on the relevant days, to help you appreciate the riches of the Christian year.

DAY BY DAY WITH GOD

Day by Day with God (published jointly with Christina Press) is written especially for women, with a regular team of contributors. Each four-monthly issue offers daily Bible readings, with key verses printed out, helpful comment, a prayer or reflection for the day ahead, and suggestions for further reading.

GUIDELINES

Guidelines is a unique Bible reading resource that offers four months of in-depth study written by leading scholars. Contributors are drawn from around the world, as well as the UK, and they represent a thought-provoking breadth of Christian tradition. *Guidelines* is written in weekly units consisting of six sections plus an introduction and a final section of points for thought and prayer.

If you would like to subscribe to one or more of these sets of Bible reading notes, please use the order form overleaf.

NOTES SUBSCRIPTIONS

☐ I would like to give a gift subscription (please complete both name and address sections below)

☐ I would like to take out a subscription myself (complete name and address details only once)

This completed coupon should be sent with appropriate payment to BRF. Alternatively, please write to us quoting your name, address, the subscription you would like for either yourself or a friend (with their name and address), the start date and credit card number, expiry date and signature if paying by credit card.

Gift subscription name _____

Gift subscription address _____

_____ Postcode _____

Please send beginning with the January / May / September issue: (delete as applicable)

(please tick box)	UK	SURFACE	AIR MAIL
NEW DAYLIGHT	☐ £12.00	☐ £13.35	☐ £15.60
GUIDELINES	☐ £12.00	☐ £13.35	☐ £15.60
DAY BY DAY WITH GOD	☐ £12.75	☐ £14.10	☐ £16.35

Please complete the payment details below and send your coupon, with appropriate payment to: **BRF, First Floor, Elsfield Hall, 15–17 Elsfield Way, Oxford OX2 8FG.**

Your name _____

Your address _____

_____ Postcode _____

Total enclosed £ _____ (cheques made payable to 'BRF')

Payment: cheque ☐ postal order ☐ Visa ☐ Mastercard ☐ Switch ☐

Card number: ☐☐☐☐☐☐☐☐☐☐☐☐☐☐☐☐

Expiry date of card: ☐☐☐☐   Issue number (Switch): ☐☐☐☐

Signature (essential if paying by credit/Switch card)

☐ Please do not send me further information about BRF publications.

BRF resources are available from your local Christian bookshop. BRF is a Registered Charity

Sometimes you need more than a card...

Bereavement
Jean Watson

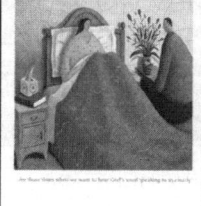
Ill Health
Wendy Bray

Marriage
Anna and Nick Brooker

Retirement
David Winter

Confirmation
Mike Starkey

Going to College
Michael Volland

Moving House
Catherine Hickey

New Baby
Lindsay Melluish

Bible Readings for Special Times are available from your local Christian bookshop or from BRF using the order form on page 32

visit www.brf.org.uk

Christian bookshops: All Christian bookshops stock BRF publications.
Telephone: To place your order, dial 01865 319700.
Fax: To place your order, dial 01865 319701.
Web: To place your order using the BRF website, visit www.brf.org.uk

REF	TITLE	PRICE	QTY	TOTAL
1 84101 418 4	Bible Readings for Special Times: Bereavement	£1.99		
1 84101 494 X	Bible Readings for Special Times: Confirmation	£1.99		
1 84101 447 8	Bible Readings for Special Times: Going to College	£1.99		
1 84101 421 4	Bible Readings for Special Times: Ill Health	£1.99		
1 84101 427 3	Bible Readings for Special Times: Marriage	£1.99		
1 84101 457 5	Bible Readings for Special Times: Moving House	£1.99		
1 84101 487 7	Bible Readings for Special Times: New Baby	£1.99		
1 84101 430 3	Bible Readings for Special Times: Retirement	£1.99		

POSTAGE & PACKING CHARGES				
Order value	UK	Europe	Surface	Air Mail
Under £7.00	£1.25	£3.00	£3.50	£5.50
£7.01–£29.99	£2.25	£5.50	£6.50	£10.00
Over £30.00	FREE	Prices on request		

Total Value of books

Postage

TOTAL

Name _____

Account Number (if known) _____

Address _____

_____ Postcode _____

Telephone _____ Email _____

❒ Please email me with information about BRF resources and services

Method of payment:
❒ Cheque ❒ Mastercard ❒ Visa ❒ Postal Order ❒ Maestro

Card no.

☐☐☐☐ ☐☐☐☐ ☐☐☐☐ ☐☐☐☐ ☐☐☐

Issue no. of Switch card ☐☐☐   Expires ☐☐ ☐☐

Shaded boxes for Maestro use only

Signature _____

Date ___/___/___

All orders must be accompanied by the appropriate payment. Please make cheques payable to BRF.

Please send your completed form to:
brf, First Floor, Elsfield Hall, 15–17 Elsfield Way, Oxford OX2 8FG

PROMO REF: BRST-GC

brf is a Registered Charity